Prophet

by Thomas Bradshaw

A Samuel French Acting Edition

Founded 1830
New York Hollywood London Toronto

SAMUELFRENCH.COM

Copyright © 2006 by Thomas Bradshaw
ALL RIGHTS RESERVED

CAUTION: Professionals and amateurs are hereby warned that *PROPHET* is subject to a licensing fee. It is fully protected under the copyright laws of the United States of America, the British Commonwealth, including Canada, and all other countries of the Copyright Union. All rights, including professional, amateur, motion picture, recitation, lecturing, public reading, radio broadcasting, television and the rights of translation into foreign languages are strictly reserved. In its present form the play is dedicated to the reading public only.

The amateur and professional live stage performance rights to *PROPHET* are controlled exclusively by Samuel French, Inc., and licensing arrangements and performance licenses must be secured well in advance of presentation. PLEASE NOTE that amateur licensing fees are set upon application in accordance with your producing circumstances. When applying for a licensing quotation and a performance license please give us the number of performances intended, dates of production, your seating capacity and admission fee. Licensing fees are payable one week before the opening performance of the play to Samuel French, Inc., at 45 W. 25th Street, New York, NY 10010.

Licensing fee of the required amount must be paid whether the play is presented for charity or gain and whether or not admission is charged.

Professional/Stock licensing fees quoted upon application to Samuel French, Inc.

For all other rights than those stipulated above, apply to: Beacon Artists Agency, 120East 56th Street, Suite 540, New York, NY 10022.

Particular emphasis is laid on the question of amateur or professional readings, permission and terms for which must be secured in writing from Samuel French, Inc.

Copying from this book in whole or in part is strictly forbidden by law, and the right of performance is not transferable.

Whenever the play is produced the following notice must appear on all programs, printing and advertising for the play: "Produced by special arrangement with Samuel French, Inc."

Due authorship credit must be given on all programs, printing and advertising for the play.

ISBN 978-0-573-63384-3   Printed in U.S.A.   #18714

> No one shall commit or authorize any act or omission by which the copyright of, or the right to copyright, this play may be impaired.

> No one shall make any changes in this play for the purpose of production.

> Publication of this play does not imply availability for performance. Both amateurs and professionals considering a production are strongly advised in their own interests to apply to Samuel French, Inc., for written permission before starting rehearsals, advertising, or booking a theatre.

> No part of this book may be reproduced, stored in a retrieval system, or transmitted in any form, by any means, now known or yet to be invented, including mechanical, electronic, photocopying, recording, videotaping, or otherwise, without the prior written permission of the publisher.

MUSIC USE NOTE

Licensees are solely responsible for obtaining formal written permission from copyright owners to use copyrighted music in the performance of this play and are strongly cautioned to do so. If no such permission is obtained by the licensee, then the licensee must use only original music that the licensee owns and controls. Licensees are solely responsible and liable for all music clearances and shall indemnify the copyright owners of the play and their licensing agent, Samuel French, Inc., against any costs, expenses, losses and liabilities arising from the use of music by licensees.

IMPORTANT BILLING AND CREDIT REQUIREMENTS

All producers of *PROPHET must* give credit to the Author of the Play in all programs distributed in connection with performances of the Play, and in all instances in which the title of the Play appears for the purposes of advertising, publicizing or otherwise exploiting the Play and/or a production. The name of the Author *must* appear on a separate line on which no other name appears, immediately following the title and *must* appear in size of type not less than fifty percent of the size of the title type.

In addition the following credit *must* be given in all programs and publicity information distributed in association with this piece:

Lyrics for Songs by Thomas Bradshaw

Music by Lois Dilivio

PROPHET was originally produced at P.S. 122 from November 30-December 17th 2005. The Stage Manager was Robin Ganek and the set design was by James Stanley with lights by Ben Kato, costumes by Iracel Shim and sound by Robert Quillen Camp. It was directed by Thomas Bradshaw and the original cast is as follows:

ALEX . . . . Peter McCabe
MONA . . . . Hilary Ketchum
JOHN . . . . Dirk Smile
MADELINE . . . . Hilary Ketchum
LISA . . . . Paula Ehrenberg
SHANIQUA . . . . Detra Payne
TYRONE . . . . Jason Grant
GOD . . . . Jerry Zellers
PRIEST . . . . Jerry Zellers
MORTICIAN . . . . Jerry Zellers
MEN . . . . Jerry Zellers, Jason Grant, Dirk Smile
FEMINIST MOB . . . . Lois Dilivio, Hilary Ketchum, Paula Ehrenberg

CHARACTERS

ALEX - A forty year old rich white lawyer
MONA - Alex's white wife
JOHN - Alex's rich black best friend
MADELINE - white, John's wife
LISA - John and Madeline's young daughter
SHANIQUA - black, A girl from the ghetto
TYRONE - black, Shaniqua's boyfriend
GOD
PRIEST
MORTICIAN
MEN
FEMINIST MOB

SETTING

Livingston, New Jersey

AUTHOR'S NOTES

All characters should be played with the utmost honesty and sincerity. The irony in the play should be underplayed rather than overplayed at all times. The characters in this play feel that all their actions are completely necessary and unavoidable. The play should be directed in a straightforward and realistic manner.

To my mother, Judythe, and my wife, Roxane, I love you.

Scene 1

ALEX. I am going to kill myself. I make myself sick.

(Pause. He's getting angry as enlightenment dawns on him.)

I have ruined my life in the most irrevocable manner for I have failed to be masculine. I have failed to rule that woman with an iron fist. She thinks that she can do anything she wants! She comes and goes as she pleases! She makes me cook and wash the dishes! She's even an independent thinker, which is the biggest sin of all!!! My father would have never tolerated this behavior from my mother. He's probably turned over in his grave every time I failed to hit that woman for not obeying me.

(He gets down on his knees and cries out:)

Forgive me god. I am unworthy of my penis. I have gone against everything that my father taught me. I know I deserve to burn in hell for my behavior. But if you give me one more chance dear lord, I promise to live my life biblically. I will live my life as Abraham and Moses did. I will be pious.

(He gives up.)

Shall I shoot myself or stab myself in the heart like a real man?

PROPHET

I understand nothing.

(His friend JOHN runs into his house frantically.)

JOHN. Alex! Your wife is dead! She's been hit by a car. I'm so sorry.
ALEX. *(Pleasantly surprised.)* Really?
JOHN. Do you think I'd joke about something like this?
ALEX. *(Getting overly excited by his good fortune.)* You're really serious?
JOHN. Aren't you upset?
ALEX. Good for her!
JOHN. What?
ALEX. Better yet, good for me.

(He starts laughing manically.)

JOHN. Sit down. You're in shock.
ALEX. I'm not in shock John.
JOHN. Then why are you so happy? You loved your wife more than anything.
ALEX. I had a revelation today. The lord revealed to me the truth of life. He revealed to me the mysteries that have eluded modern humanity for so long. We need to lead our lives as Abraham and Moses did.
JOHN. What are you talking about?
ALEX. I can't tell you how to live, rather I will lead by example. That's how the prophets of old did things.
JOHN. How do you know? You've only been to church once, and that was for your wedding.
ALEX. Fuck you. I know what I used to say, but now I've had a revelation. Don't get snotty with me just because you're jealous that

PROPHET

god revealed the truth of life to me and not you.
    JOHN. I'm not jealous Alex.
    ALEX. Sure you're not.

(ALEX winks at JOHN.)

    JOHN. I'm not!
    ALEX. You don't have to tell me twice.
    JOHN. I'm just concerned about your sanity.
    ALEX. I'll wait until you calm down before I resume my preaching. Anyway, where's her body?
    JOHN. She was lying in the middle of the road about three blocks away.
    ALEX. Let's try to get there before the ambulance arrives. I want to make sure that there's no chance that she'll be revived.

(JOHN shakes his head and they run out of the door.)

End Scene

Scene 2

(At rise ALEX is at the morgue.)

    MORTICIAN. I'm sorry for your loss.
    ALEX. Thank you. It's been hard but life goes on.

(MORTICIAN slides the body out.)

MORTICIAN. That's a good attitude to have.

ALEX. Is it alright if I spend a few moments alone with her to say goodbye? *(He looks as if he's going to break down.)* It happened so suddenly.

MORTICIAN. Certainly. It's important to have closure.

ALEX. She's beautiful isn't she? She looks like an angel.

MORTICIAN. She's very beautiful. I'll leave you two alone now.

(MORTICIAN leaves.)

ALEX. *(Leans in close to her and strokes her face.)* You stupid bitch. You got exactly what you deserved. This is the first useful thing you've done for me. You were nothing but a weight that held me down, and prevented me from dancing in the beautiful scorching rays of the sun. *(He spits in her face. Pause.)* Thank you, God, for this magnificent new lease on life. I was once a non-believer but now I understand your awesome power. *(He turns back to his wife.)* You should have done the dishes more. May you burn in hell you frigid cunt.

VOICE OF GOD. 1865.

ALEX. What?

VOICE OF GOD. 1865.

ALEX. What does that mean oh mighty lord?

VOICE OF GOD. It's the year that humanity lost its way.

ALEX. I still don't understand.

VOICE OF GOD. Think about it.

ALEX. You're not being clear.

VOICE OF GOD. Get used to it.

(Pause.)

PROPHET

VOICE OF GOD. O.K. I'll give you a hint. Find yourself a woman.
ALEX. Thank you for your kindness and wisdom great lord.
VOICE OF GOD. Anytime.
ALEX. *(ALEX ponders God's word for a moment.)* Find myself a woman? 1865? What does this all mean? *(He pauses and ponders the Lord's word again. ALEX finally figures out the Lord's riddle.)*

(Music Starts and ALEX bursts into song.)

I'M GONNA MARY A NEGRESS
A NEGRESS IS THE ONE FOR ME
NO MORE SMART INTELLIGENT WHITE WOME
AN ILLITERATE WOMAN SUITS MY NEEDS

I'M GONNA MARY A NEGRESS
HAVE A STRICT DIET OF MCDONALD'S AND KFC
EAT SOME WATERMELON AND CHITLINS
A BUSHY PUSSY'S THE PLACE TO BE

I'M GONNA MARY A NEGRESS
CAUSE THOSE BLACKS LIKE TO SUCK AND FUCK LIKE
   DOGS IN HEAT
THEY'RE BASICALLY JUST LIKE MONEKYS
'CEPT THEY DON'T EVEN KNOW WHERE TO PEE

I'M GONNA MARY A NEGRESS
AND SMOKE SOME CRACK WHILE I ENJOY THE BREEZ
NO MORE SMART INTELLIGENT WHITE WOMEN
GONNA EAT SOME WATERMELON AND CHITLINS
GONNA GRAB THE BACK OF HER HEAD

PROPHET

WHILE SHE SUCKS ME OFF IN THE BATHROOM OF RED LOBSTER

End Scene

Scene 3

(At rise a beautiful black woman in a tight jumpsuit is strutting around on stage when ALEX ENTERS. ALEX has gone to the ghetto of Newark, New Jersey.)

ALEX. What are you up to baby. *(She ignores him.)* You sure do look fine. I wouldn't mind seeing what's beneath your clothes.
SHANIQUA. You got weak game. You beta keep on walkin.
ALEX. I don't have weak game.
SHANIQUA. Yes you do.
ALEX. No I don't.
SHANIQUA. Yes you do nigga.
ALEX. What did you call me?
SHANIQUA. You heard me.
ALEX. But I'm not black.
SHANIQUA. Dat don't change nothin.
ALEX. If you say so. What's your name?
SHANIQUA. Shaniqua.
ALEX. That's a beautiful name. I bet you were an African Queen in a past life.
SHANIQUA. *(She laughs.)* Dat's sweet. What your name?
ALEX. Alex.

PROPHET

SHANIQUA. How much money you got?
ALEX. What do you mean?
SHANIQUA. You got a job?
ALEX. Oh yes, I'm a lawyer.
SHANIQUA. Dat's what I'm talkin bout. I need a man like you. A man who can take care uv me. I'm sick of my nappy headed losa.
ALEX. Do you have a boyfriend?
SHANIQUA. Yeah, but he ain't all dat.
ALEX. What does he do for a living?
SHANIQUA. He deal drugs.
ALEX. *(Excited.)* What kind?
SHANIQUA. Crack. Why? You want some?
ALEX. *(Disappointed.)* No. I was hoping he sold cocaine.
SHANIQUA. Is you crazy? We don't got no Coke round here! Dat a white man's drug. Can't nobody afford dat stuff round here.
ALEX. Will you go out with me?
SHANIQUA. Only if you take me classy places, like Red Lobster and Bennigan's.
ALEX. No problem.
SHANIQUA. *(They kiss.)* I like you.
ALEX. You're exactly the kind of girl that I've been looking for.

(They kiss again and start to walk offstage when TYRONE ENTERS.)

TYRONE. Where you think you goin Bitch!?
SHANIQUA. I ain't yo property!
TYRONE. Oh yes you is.
SHANIQUA. I don't see no ring on my finga.
ALEX. *(Coming between them.)* She's mine now. Step off.
TYRONE. *(To SHANIQUA.)* Who's dis stupid craka?
SHANIQUA. I don't need you no mo. I got a new man.

PROPHET

TYRONE. *(Pulls out a gun and puts it to her head.)* Stop bein foolish you stupid Ho. Rememba dat I'm de daddy uv yo kids.

SHANIQUA. You only de daddy of two my kids.

TYRONE. *(Hurt.)* What? I thought I was de daddy uv all five!

SHANIQUA. Nope. And de one I'm pregnant wid now ain't yo's eitha.

TYRONE. *(Points the gun at ALEX.)* Don't tell me dat dis craka is de daddy uv dis one.

SHANIQUA. Nope. James from Clark street de Daddy.

TYRONE. *(Police sirens are heard. Begging.)* Please don't tell no one bout dis. I'll lose all respec on de street if my boys find out that all yo kids ain't mine.

SHANIQUA. I'll try.

(TYRONE runs offstage because of the sirens.)

TYRONE. Thanks.

End of Scene

Scene 4

(At rise ALEX and SHANIQUA are walking into ALEX's house.)

SHANIQUA. Dinna was amazin.

ALEX. You have quite the appetite. I really didn't think that you'd be able to eat 75 popcorn shrimp, but you proved me wrong.

SHANIQUA. I normally can't, but de shrimp was so good. De

PROPHET

chef at Red Lobster mus be famous.

ALEX. Perhaps. *(Pause.)* Tyrone seems like a tough guy.

SHANIQUA. He not. He jus like to act all tough and macho. He really sweet once you get to know him, sort uv like a teddy bear.

ALEX. He put a gun to your head and *mine*.

SHANIQUA. Don be mindin dat. He be pointin' dat gun at me all de time. I don even be payin attention to dat no mo.

ALEX. Do you think that he'd hurt me?

SHANIQUA. Don't even trip. I already tol you. Dat fool be pointin dat gun at everyone.

ALEX. If you say so. *(Pause.)* Where do you and your kids live?

SHANIQUA. Wid my mama. Only two my kids live wid me.

ALEX. *(Visibly Surprised.)* It's good to see young minority youth taking responsibility for their actions! Most minority youth impregnate women and don't take care of their kids! But you found men that help you raise them!

SHANIQUA. My otha three kids don't be stayin wid dey daddies.

ALEX. They stay with their grandmothers then?

SHANIQUA. No. Dey was taken away by social services.

ALEX. For what?

SHANIQUA. Dey said Dat I was neglectin my children. But I wasn't. I fed and cloth them. A girl's gotta hav fun sometimes. Social Services got all angry just 'cause me and my moms would go to de club togetha and leave de kids home alone.

ALEX. I guess you and your mother are close.

SHANIQUA. Yeah we close. We kinda like sistas. We'd leave de oldest one in charge. *(With conviction.)* Ain't nothin wrong wid dat.

ALEX. That doesn't sound so bad. How old is your oldest?

SHANIQUA. Eight. When I was eight I took care uv my brothas

and sistas.
ALEX. I see. And how old are you.
SHANIQUA. How old you think I am?
ALEX. I'm not sure, but I know that you're the most beautiful girl that I've ever met.
SHANIQUA. Oh.

(They Kiss deeply.)

ALEX. So, how old are you?
SHANIQUA. Twenty-Three.

(ALEX calculates how old she was when she had her first child in his head.)

ALEX. I remember when I was Twenty-three. Youthful, virile, in my prime.
SHANIQUA. What do "virile" mean?
ALEX. You'll find out soon enough. I'm quite virile for a man my age.
SHANIQUA. How old you is?
ALEX. Forty.
SHANIQUA. For real? I'd neva guess dat. I thought you was in yo late twenties. You look good. *(They start seriously making out and taking their clothes off when ALEX stops.)* What's wrong?
ALEX. There are some things that I want you to wear.
SHANIQUA. *(She is very excited by this prospect.)* Lingerie? I like dat. You a real classy guy.
ALEX. I wouldn't exactly call it lingerie.
SHANIQUA. Ohh, you makin me wet. I bet you into somethin real kinky. I love kinky. You know what really be turnin me on?

PROPHET

(Things are really getting heated between them. She is stroking his penis through his pants.)

ALEX. What?
SHANIQUA. Anal sex. I love when guys be fukin me in de ass. It make me cum ova and ova again.
ALEX. I'm gonna fuck you in the ass so hard that you're gonna bleed.
SHANIQUA. Yeah, keep talkin dirty to me. I love it.
ALEX. I will. After you put on your new clothes.
SHANIQUA. I don't know if I can wait. I need you to fuck me right now. Feel my wetness.

(She sticks his hand down her pants and pulls it out after he feels her wetness. He then licks his finger.)

ALEX. You taste like rosewater.

(He gets up and comes back with tattered slave clothing and shackles.)

SHANIQUA. *(SHANIQUA is perplexed.)* What are dose? Dat ain't lingerie. Dose clothes look a hunred years old.
ALEX. It would mean so much to me if you'd put these clothes on. It would make me so hot to see your luscious curves in these.
SHANIQUA. *(Warming up to the idea.)* Oh I see, you into some weird bondage shit. I love bein tied up, love when guys be real rough wid me. Remind me uv my daddy.
ALEX. Put them on. Your mine now. *(She finishes removing her clothing and he puts on the tattered slave clothing.)* You look beautiful.

PROPHET

(He then clasps the chains around her hands and feet.)

SHANIQUA. I need you to fuck me so bad.

(ALEX is now holding her from behind with his pelvis pressed against her in a very sexual manner.)

ALEX. *(Sweetly.)* Now you're everything that a woman should be.

SHANIQUA. Fuck me.

(ALEX is overcome with lust and love and throws her face down on the couch. He then violently rips open her shirt and lifts up her skirt. He then pulls out his penis and starts to have sex with her.)

ALEX. You feel so good. You're a real woman. I love you. *(He ejaculates.)*

SHANIQUA. *(Panting and gasping.)* I love you too.

End Of Scene

PROPHET

Scene 5
*Song: **Oh How Sweet and Beautiful Love Is.***

(This song should be sung straight, like an old-fashioned love duet.)

SHANIQUA.
OH HOW SWEET AND BEAUTIFUL LOVE IS
I'VE PRAYED MY WHOLE LIFE FOR THIS DAY
ALEX IS THE KINDEST MAN ALIVE
HE SUITS MY NEEDS IN EVERY WAY

ALEX.
OH HOW STRANGE AND MYSTICAL LIFE IS
GOD SPOKE AND TRANSFORMED ME INTO A PROPHET YESTERDAY
THEN SENT ME THE MOST BEAUTIFUL ANGEL FROM HEAVEN
TO LIGHT THE REST OF MY DAYS

SHANIQUA.
OH HOW WONDEROUS AND UNPREDICTABLE LIFE IS
I WAS JUST A LONELY GIRL FROM THE GHETTO YESTERDAY
STRUGGLING TO BE THE BEST MOTHER I COULD
DREAMING FOR A MAN LIKE ALEX TO COME MY WAY

ALEX.
OH HOW SCORCHING YET GENTLE THE WORLD CAN BE
CHANCE COMES AND GIVES AND TAKES AT WILL
YESTERDAY I WAS MARRIED TO A TYRANT FROM HELL
TODAY LIFE IS PERFECT AND I BASK IN THE RAIN'S MYSTICAL HAZE

PROPHET

BOTH.
NOW WE HAVE EACH OTHER

SHANIQUA. ALEX.
WE WILL NEVER KNOW SADNESS OR LONLINESS

BOTH
AGAIN.

SHANIQUA.
YESTERDAY WE WERE NOTHING
BUT DISTRAUGHT SOULS
DRIFTING THROUGH LIFE

ALEX.
TOGETHER WE WILL START A FAMILY

BOTH.
AND BE EACH OTHER'S JOY
FOR THE REST OF OUR DAYS,
FOR THE REST OF OUR DAYS

SHANIQUA. ALEX.
OH HOW SWEET AND BEAU- OH HOW STRANGE
TIFUL LOVE IS AND MYSTICAL!
HOW I'VE PRAYED MY GOD SPOKE AND NOW
WHOLE LIFE FOR THIS DAY I'M A PROPHET
ALEX IS THE KINDEST MAN YOU'RE MY HEAVENLY
ALIVE ANGEL
HE SUITS MY NEEDS IN
EVERY WAY

PROPHET

OH HOW WONDROUS! LONELY GIRL FROM THE GHETTO STRUGGLING TO BE A GOOD MOM	OH HOW SCORCHING YET GENTLE THE WORLD CAN BE CHANCE COMES AND GIVES AND TAKES AT WILL YESTERDAY I WAS MARRIED TO A TYRANT FROM HELL TODAY LIFE IS PERFECT AND I BASK IN THE RAIN'S MYSTICAL HAZE.
DREAMING OF A MAN LIKE ALEX TO COME MY WAY	YOU'RE AN ANGEL WHO LIGHTS THE REST OF MY DAYS

BOTH.
YOU SUIT MY NEEDS IN EVERY WAY

(The song transforms into wedding music and a priest comes onstage. Wedding bells are heard.)

PRIEST. Do you Shaniqua take Alex to be your lawfully wedded husband?
SHANIQUA. I do.
PRIEST. Do you Alex take Shaniqua to be your lawfully wedded wife?
ALEX. I do.

(They exchange rings.)

PROPHET

PRIEST. I now pronounce you man and wife. You may kiss the bride.

(They kiss and cheers are heard.)

End Of Scene

Scene 6

(At rise SHANIQUA and ALEX are talking in their house.)

SHANIQUA. What was yo wife like?
ALEX. She was a hard woman to live with.
SHANIQUA. In what way?
ALEX. Let me tell you a story.

(Lights dim on SHANIQUA and ALEX. ALEX ENTERS the room to find his wife MONA ignoring him. He goes over to her.)

ALEX. Hey honey, what's wrong?
MONA. You didn't clean the floor the way I asked you to.
ALEX. Yes I did!

MONA. *(Putting the toothbrush in his face.)* I told you to use this toothbrush. The package isn't even open.

ALEX. But I got on my hands and knees and scrubbed it. We have different methods, but the result is the same. *(MONA is on the verge of tears. He puts his arms around her and starts kissing her*

PROPHET

neck.) I'm sorry.
 MONA. What are you doing?
 ALEX. I thought that maybe making love would make things better.
 MONA. Better for who?
 ALEX. Better for us. We need to connect
 MONA. I don't feel like it.
 ALEX. It's been over a month.
 MONA. I'm sick of your penis. I will not have my life ruled by it.
 ALEX. Please honey. I washed all the dishes, vacuumed every rug in the house, cleaned the windows-
 MONA. *(Breaking down.)* But you didn't clean the floor the way I like! It's because you hate me.
 ALEX. *(Consoling.)* Fine. If it means that much to you I'll clean it again the way you like. I'm sorry. *(They kiss.)* Do you feel better now?

(She nods her head yes like an innocent puppy dog. They start kissing again and she abruptly pulls away.)

 MONA. *(Sternly, with absolute conviction.)* Not until you clean the damn floor properly!
 ALEX. *(Pathetic and hurt.)* O.K. Honey.

(He gets down on the floor and starts cleaning it with the toothbrush. Lights fade and the lights come back up on SHANIQUA and ALEX. She is cradling him through her chains.)

 SHANIQUA. I'm so sorry you had to go through dat. She sound like a real witch. I can't believe you had to deal wid dat for all dose yeas. How long was you two married for?
 ALEX. Fifteen years.
 SHANIQUA. Dat all ova now baby. You don't neva hav to deal

wid her nonsense again. Why don't we have some nice anal sex. Would dat make my poor pookie happy?

(ALEX shakes his head up and down excitedly like a little boy.)

ALEX. Then we have to go to the funeral.

(ALEX throws her on the couch and proceeds to Rip her shirt open and flip her skirt up like he did before. Lights fade to black while they're having very violent anal sex.)

End Scene

Scene 7

(At rise it is MONA's funeral. They are at the grave. SHANIQUA, JOHN, ALEX, PRIEST, and MONA are onstage.)

PRIEST. We gather here today to lay to rest one of the kindest souls that has ever walked the earth. I thank the good Lord that I had the pleasure to know her during her short but compassionate life. We should all try to lead our lives the way Mona led hers. Blah Blah Blah. She's in heaven holding Jesus's hand right now. Blah Blah Blah. I fucked her once.

ALEX. What the fuck are you doing?

(MONA throws open the Coffin.)

PROPHET

EVERYONE EXCEPT ALEX AND SHANIQUA. Happy April Fool's Day!

(Everyone starts clapping and laughing except ALEX and SHANIQUA. They were all in on the joke.)

JOHN. *(Patting ALEX on the back.)* We sure got you!
MONA. Aren't you happy to see me Alex? Aren't you happy that your smoochie's not dead?
ALEX. Oh no you don't!
MONA. Don't tell me you're upset. I was sure you'd think it was funny.
PRIEST. How'd you like my comment about having fucked her? Get it? I'm a priest. I'd never do something like that.

(Everyone laughs.)

ALEX. You probably wouldn't. But you'd probably fuck one of these little boys here.
SHANIQUA. Alex! Watch yo mouth! We in public!
ALEX. Shut up Woman!
MONA. Apologize to him! He's a holy man.
ALEX. You're not gonna do this to me.
MONA. Do what?
ALEX. Ruin my life again. *(He shouts out to GOD.)* Why have you forsaken me dear lord? I was so happy?
GOD. I don't know.
ALEX. What do you mean you don't know? You're God. I thought you knew everything.
GOD. I just do things sometimes. It's a test. Yes that's it. Remember how I had Jesus fester in the desert for forty days and forty

nights while Satan taunted and tempted him. I even had him strung up and nailed to a cross! And he was my son! You should feel privileged that this is all I'm doing to you.

ALEX. You're right dear lord, but why? Why? Why?

GOD. To make sure you're loyal. I don't like fickle souls. I want to make sure you believe in my word and preach what I say. By the way, you've been doing a great job so far. You married a good woman and she's dressed quite well. You definitely got the message.

MONA. What? I die for two days and you go off and marry some nigger. How could you?

ALEX. You made my life hell for fifteen years. Shaniqua has made me happy for the first time in my life.

JOHN. You married her?

ALEX. *(To Mona.)* I will not stand for you coming back and making my life hell again. I'm a prophet now. I have a woman who truly loves me and knows how to obey my word. I'm gonna pass this test.

SHANIQUA. *(He rushes over to the coffin and strangles her.)* Alex, stop chokin her!

(MONA dies.)

SHANIQUA. Damn.
GOD. Good Job! You passed the test.

End Of Scene

PROPHET

Scene 8

(At rise ALEX and Shaniqua are alone on stage holding each other lovingly when the doorbell rings. ALEX answers the door. It is JOHN.)

ALEX. Come in.

(JOHN ENTERS and ALEX and JOHN stare at each other for a few moments.)

JOHN. I'm so sorry that I didn't believe that you're a prophet.
ALEX. *(To SHANIQUA.)* Go stand in the corner and cover your ears.
SHANIQUA. Why?
ALEX. Do it.
SHANIQUA. Why can't I jus go upstairs?
ALEX. Cause you can't be trusted on your own. Now go in the corner and cover your ears before I get nasty. *(SHANIQUA goes in the corner and covers her ears.)* Fucking women.

(He turns and stares at JOHN in a menacing manner.)

JOHN. I also realize that the April Fool's joke wasn't very funny.
ALEX. It was completely fucked up!
JOHN. Please forgive me, but we all thought that you'd get a big kick out of it! You've always loved that kind of stuff.
ALEX. You betrayed me. But I'm going to forgive you as Jesus would have. Being a prophet has made me see things in a different light.
JOHN. C'mon, admit that you would've thought it was funny if you hadn't had that revelation.

PROPHET

ALEX. Pause. *(ALEX smiles.)* You're right. I probably would have been dying of laughter if I hadn't had that revelation.

JOHN. How could I predict your sudden change of heart?

ALEX. It was a pretty good April Fool's joke.

(They Hug.)

JOHN. *(He's looking at SHANIQUA.)* Where did you find her?

ALEX. In the ghetto.

JOHN. My wife would never do that. I want to get me one of those.

ALEX. Let's jump in the car and get you one right now.

(They start to rush out the door when god speaks.)

GOD. Wait!

ALEX. What's wrong?

GOD. You're a damn idiot!

ALEX. I'm just trying to fulfill your miraculous will lord!

GOD. You misinterpreted my vague and misleading hints stupid! I don't want you to just enslave nigger- I mean Black-no that's not right- African American women! All women must be controlled! You must lead the revolution. This is your duty. The world has turned to complete chaos! Look at yourself John!

JOHN. *(Afraid.)* What have I done?

GOD. Look how you treat your wife! It's disgusting! Did men cook in the bible? Did men let their wives out of their sight for one moment in the bible? You men have gone crazy! Do you hear? There's a reason I created Eve from Adam's bone. I did it to show his superiority. Claim back manhood or I'm sending all men to hell! All of you! I've got to get going.

ALEX and JOHN. Bye God.

PROPHET

JOHN. What am I going to do? My wife's not gonna like this too much.

ALEX. You can do it John! I did it!

JOHN. You can't compare our situations.

ALEX. Yes I can.

JOHN. No you can't! I've got an educated white woman on my hands who also happens to be a feminist! What do you have? A stupid nigger from the Ghetto! She was already a slave.

SHANIQUA. What did he just call me?

ALEX. Cover your ears tighter! *(To JOHN, threatening.)* Don't talk about her that way. She's my wife. I love her dearly.

JOHN. I'm sorry.

ALEX. It's o.k. I'll be right back. I've got to go get something for you.

(He leaves the room and comes back with a tattered slave outfit and chains.)

JOHN. Oh no.

ALEX. Oh yes. You're gonna go home right now and tell your wife that she's putting this on.

JOHN. I can't. I'm scared.

ALEX. Do you want to go to hell?

JOHN. Alright, I'll do it.

ALEX. Good luck and god bless you.

End Of Scene

PROPHET

Scene 9

(At rise JOHN has entered his house and speaks to his wife.)

JOHN. *(Meekly.)* Hey Honey. What's wrong?
MADELINE. You didn't wash the dishes John. I told you to wash the dishes.
JOHN. Sorry honey, I was in a rush.
MADELINE. Hmmph!
JOHN. Don't be mad. I'll wash them right now. *(JOHN goes to wash the dishes, then he suddenly remembers his task and gets a hold of himself and turns to her defiantly.)* You wash the goddamn dishes woman!
MADELINE. What did you say to me?
JOHN. You heard me! I'm putting you in your place like Moses and Abraham would have done.
MADELINE. *(Pause.)* Have you been taking LSD?
JOHN. No!

(She feels his head.)

MADELINE. I'm taking you to the hospital. Mental illness runs in your family.

(She puts on her Jacket and Frantically looks for her keys.)

JOHN. You're not taking me anywhere. The only thing you're going to do is put on these.

(He shows her the tattered slave clothing and the chains.)

MADELINE. What are those for?

PROPHET

JOHN. I am enslaving you as god has decreed.
MADELINE. No you're not!

(MADELINE kicks JOHN in the balls.)

JOHN. Yes I am!

(He grabs her hair and they violently struggle through the next few lines.)

MADELINE. No!
JOHN. Yes!
MADELINE. No!
JOHN. Yes!
MADELINE. No!
JOHN. Yes!

(Their daughter LISA ENTERS.)

LISA. *(She Screams)* Stop killing mommy!

(They both stop struggling.)

JOHN. I'm not killing Mommy. I'm on a mission from GOD.
MADELINE. A mission from god!? Have you been talking to Alex?
JOHN. Alex is a prophet now. You'd do well to heed his word.
MADELINE. Yeah well I've got a prophecy too. You guys will find out about my prophecy later.

(She EXITS.)

PROPHET

LISA. So god wants you to kill mommy?

JOHN. No. God just wants women to be the way they were in the bible, and if daddy doesn't help god out, then daddy's going to go to hell.

LISA. I don't want you to go to hell. What do women in the bible have to do?

JOHN. They have to wear these clothes and chains and obey their husbands' every command.

LISA. Does that mean that I have to wear those clothes too?

JOHN. *(He is confused. He never thought of this.)* Good question. I don't know sweetie.

End Of Scene

Scene 10

(At rise ALEX is preaching to a group of men in Livingston, New Jersey. Perhaps the men could simply be a recording. Or maybe there are a just couple of men on stage. ALEX should deliver this like a sermon. It should have the feeling of a Christian revival. When there are multiple lines for the men, the sentences should be staggered.)

ALEX. Are you hot blooded Christian American Men?

MEN. Hell Yeah!

ALEX. Do you believe in the holy word of the bible?

MEN. Of course!

ALEX. Do you believe deep in your hearts that the bible is the

PROPHET

ultimate human law?

MEN. *(Loud Cheering.)* Yeah! Yeah! God is great! Jesus is Great! God is great! Jesus is great-

(ALEX Cuts them off.)

ALEX. If you believe in biblical law then why don't you follow it?

MEN. *(MEN are confused.)* What? What's he talking about? I think I followed the bible. I haven't slept with my dog or my daughter. I think that's one of the ten commandments.

ALEX. I'll tell you why! Because you all act like faggots! So go on! Go to the gay pride parade and march like the homos that you are!

MEN. I'm not a homo! I'll show you who's a homo! I'm gonna fuck you up man!

ALEX. If you want to prove that you're not a bunch of faggots then you need to take your manhood back! You need to go home and put your wives in their places! You need to stop letting them run your lives!

MEN. *(Wild Cheering.)* Alright! Yeah!

ALEX. Genesis says that Eve was made from Adam's rib. That means that women are inferior to men! *(Wild Cheering.)* Do you know what the prefix Wo means? The prefix Wo means less than. Therefore the word Woman means less than man! *(Wild Cheering.)* Men need to start living as Moses and Abraham did in the bible! Did Moses and Abraham take their wives opinions into consideration?

MEN. No!

ALEX. Did Moses and Abraham let their wives out of their sights for one minute?

MEN. No!

ALEX. Damn right they didn't! It's fucking heresy! Do you

know why?

MEN. Why?

ALEX. You know why?

MEN. Why?

ALEX. Say it louder! I can't hear you! I want to hear the spirit reverberate through your voices!

MEN. *(With Soul.)* Why Brother?

ALEX. Cause Eve ate the forbidden fruit from the tree of knowledge while Adam wasn't looking. Women can't be trusted! Those sluts have been being dishonest and ruining the lives of men since the beginning of time! *(Wild Cheering.)* They must be put back in their places!

MEN. Put them back! Put them back! Put them back! Put them back! Put them back! Put them back!

ALEX. *(He quiets the men.)* Do you want to meet the ideal woman? *(More Wild Cheering.)* I present you with Shaniqua! *(SHANIQUA comes out on stage. The men fall silent.)* Do not be afraid. God, the lord himself directed me to treat her as such. He has entrusted me with the sacred mission to bring order back to the world. God wants each of you to go home and enslave your wives in this manner.

MEN. What if I don't want to? I don't think my wife will like this very much. Can't we---

ALEX. Then you shall burn in hell for all eternity! I have attire for each of your wives. So take one as you leave. God bless you all! And good luck!

MEN. *(Cheering.)* Hail Saint Alex! Hail to the Prophet! Hail Saint Alex! Hail to the Prophet!

(The men leave and only JOHN and SHANIQUA are left.)

ALEX. Did you see that John? Soon god's commandments shall

PROPHET

be fulfilled.
JOHN. I have to ask you a question.
ALEX. Speak your troubles brother.
JOHN. You say that all women must be enslaved.
ALEX. That's right.
JOHN. Does that mean that I must enslave my daughter also?
ALEX. *(Perturbed.)* Good question.

(They look up at the sky towards God as if they are awaiting an answer. As they're waiting, a mob of feminists run on stage led by JOHN's wife MADELINE.)

MADELINE. There they are! Let's castrate them!

(They chase JOHN and ALEX off stage.)

End Scene

Scene 11

(At rise ALEX, JOHN, and SHANIQUA ENTER after having been chased away by the feminists. They are at ALEX and SHANIQUA's home.)

JOHN. That was close.
ALEX. Sure was. Did you see how excited those men were? The men of Livingston, New Jersey are finally going to take their lives back. And after the men of Livingston start living biblically

PROPHET

we'll take our message to all the men of New Jersey, and then we'll run commercials broadcasting our message nationally like Billy Graham, and then-
  JOHN. Alex. I have a-
  ALEX. Don't ever cut me off again! I'm laying out my vision to you! *(Tries to go back to what he was saying before.)* And then- And then we're going to take our message-Hmm. Look what you've done! I've lost my train of thought. *(Pause.)* You may speak now.
  SHANIQUA. I gotta go to de bathroom.
  ALEX. Don't take too long.

(She EXITS.)

  JOHN. This is really hard. Madeline won't wear her chains.
  ALEX. What do you mean she won't? She doesn't have a choice. You have to make her.
  JOHN. I tried! I literally wrestled her to the ground. She thought I was high on LSD and tried to take me to the hospital. Didn't you see that she was leading that mob of feminists?
  ALEX. No. *(Pause.)* This is tough. I didn't expect to encounter so much resistance. *(Pause.)* We might have to resort to violence.
  JOHN. What kind?

(SHANIQUA ENTERS. SHE has removed her chains.)

  ALEX. Where are your chains?!
  SHANIQUA. I cut them off. They was hurtin me.
  ALEX. *(In Disbelief.)* Did I give you permission to take off your chains?
  SHANIQUA. I was uncomftable. I don need yo pamission to fell comftable!

PROPHET

(She snaps her finger at him in defiance.)

ALEX. I can't believe this!

SHANIQUA. Well believe it! When dis all started I jus thought dat it was a kinky game you was playin. You was sweet to me even if you was weird. You made my pussy wet all de time and I be lovin de way you fuck me up de ass. *(Pause.)* But dis has gone too far Alex. I ain't gonna play dis game no mo. You scary now. You no longa the sweet gentle man dat I married. I want dis marriage to work out. But I gonna leave if you keep dragin me around in dese chains all day!

ALEX. I'm very disappointed in you. I thought you were different from all the other women I've dated. All those educated, cold, white, feminists. But now I see that you're the same. I thought you knew your place, but now I see that you don't. *(Pause.)* Put your chains back on.

SHANIQUA. I leavin Alex. You scarin me.

(She tries to leave.)

ALEX. *(He blocks her.)* You're not going anywhere you damned bitch!

SHANIQUA. Let me go!

ALEX. You're going to learn how to obey me right now. You're going to learn how to accept the word of the Lord our God. *(To JOHN.)* Restrain her while I get something from the next room.

(JOHN is in shock. HE restrains HER and ALEX leaves the room. ALEX comes back with a Bull whip from the time of Slavery. ALEX Grabs SHANIQUA roughly and chains her to the wall.)

SHANIQUA. Please don't do dis Alex! I promise I'll be a good

PROPHET

girl.

ALEX. Too late. We're going to do this old school. Chain her up, John. *(ALEX rips off her shirt and proceeds to whip her. She screams violently. He lashes her about ten times. Each time we hear the cracking of the whip. Perhaps this part of the scene should be performed using a strobe light. ALEX shouts Obcenities while he whips her.)* This will teach you you stupid nigger bitch!

> You will feel god's wrath.
> God's wrath is raining upon you like a sea of arrows.
> May enough of your blood spill to fill a river.
> I only do this because I love you.

(The whipping ends.)

I hope this will teach you to obey the word of god you stupid bitch.

(ALEX presents JOHN with his own whip.)

This is how you're going to make your wife obey you.

(JOHN takes the whip. JOHN is reluctant. He is horrified by what he just saw Alex do.)

Good luck brother! May god be with you!

End Scene

PROPHET

Scene 12

(SHANIQUA and ALEX are in opposite parts of the house alone. SHANIQUA is back in her chains. They sing.)

ALEX.
I THOUGHT SHE WAS MY PERFECT WOMAN
I LEARNED THE SAD TRUTH TODAY
SHE'S NOT THAT MUCH DIFFERENT
FROM MY DEAD WIFE MONA WHO RUINED MY LIFE IN
  EVERY WAY

SHANIQUA.
I THOUGHT HE WAS A PRINCE
HE SWEPT ME FROM THE GHETTO AND BROUGHT ME TO
  LIVE IN HIS MANSION
BUT NOW I KNOW HE'S A TERRIBLE TYRANT
AND THAT MONEY CAN'T MAKE YOU HAPPY

ALEX.
DOES MY PERFECT WOMAN EXIST?
WHY CAN'T SHE BE WHO I WANT HER TO BE?
I DIDN'T WANT TO WHIP HER LIKE THAT
BUT I CAN'T CHANGE WHAT GOD HAS DECREED

SHANIQUA.
I WISH I WAS BACK IN NEWARK WITH TYRONE
NOW I SEE THAT HE TREATED MY PRETTY GREAT
SOMETIMES YOU CAN'T SEE WHAT YOU HAD UNTIL
  YOU'VE LEFT IT BEHIND
 I WISH I COULD CHANGE THE PAST

PROPHET

SHANIQUA + ALEX.
HELP ME TO FIND MY WAY LORD
HELP ME TO HAVE THE STRENGTH
TO HELP ME TO GO ON LIVING
AND ESCAPE THIS TERRIBLE PAIN

WHY CAN'T SHE/HE CHANGE LORD?
AND HE WHO I WANT HER/HIM TO BE?
AND TREAT ME LIKE HE/SHE USED TO
AND BE MY SOUL MATE THROUGH THE REST OF MY DAYS

(End of song. ALEX EXITS the stage. TYRONE ENTERS through the window loudly.)

SHANIQUA. Tyrone! Stop makin all dat racket! What you doin here anyway?

TYRONE. I'm takin you back! Dats what I'm doin! I'm de laughin stock uv de hood because you ran off wid dat Craka!

SHANIQUA. Shh! I don't want Alex to hear you!

TYRONE. I don't care whether he hear me! I ain't takin no for an answer. You my Bitch. I own you no matta what dat craka say!

SHANIQUA. I want to go wid you.

TYRONE. Really?

SHANIQUA. I've missed you so much baby. I'm so sorry I left. I love you.

TYRONE. Oh baby. I missed you too. I been beatin my dick every night thinkin about yo sweet ass. About de way you lick my balls and let me come all ova yo face. *(They kiss and rub against one another for a little while. He sees her back.)* What de fuck?

SHANIQUA. C'mon. Let's go befo Alex hear us.

(They start to go out the window when ALEX ENTERS.)

PROPHET

ALEX. What's the meaning of this? I can't leave you alone for one minute. This is why I don't let you out of my sight you fucking cunt! You're just like Eve. If Adam had kept an eye on Eve then there wouldn't be all this sin in the world today.

TYRONE. What kind of nonsense is you talkin?

ALEX. *(To TYRONE.)* Get out of my house you monkey.

TYRONE. What did you call me? I'll fuck you up!

ALEX. You heard me. Go back to the ghetto and deal your drugs.

TYRONE. I'm takin Shaniqua! She my woman.

ALEX. No you're not!

TYRONE. *(TYRONE takes out his gun and points it at ALEX.)* Oh yes I is you pasty faced craka! Up in here lookin like a ghost!

ALEX. I'm not afraid of your gun. *(He moves closer to TYRONE.)* I'm a prophet. God is on my side. I'm invincible!

(He stretches out his arms imitating the sign of the cross.)

TYRONE. *(To SHANIQUA.)* Dis nigga is whacked out! What kind of shit he be smokin? Dis niggas talkin crazy!

ALEX. I'm not your nigger!

SHANIQUA. Alex! Don't make Tyrone shoot you. I'm goin wid him. You can't stop me. Jus let me go.

ALEX. Your bullets can't hurt me!

(He moves closer to Tyrone.)

TYRONE. Get back! I'll shoot you muthafuka! I'll make you my fifty-third murder victim!

GOD. Tyrone! This is God. I order you not to shoot Alex. He is my prophet!

TYRONE. What de hell? Is dere some crazy sound system in here?

ALEX. No! I told you. God will protect me! Thank you great lord.

(ALEX tries to grab TYRONE's gun and they struggle for a while. TYRONE eventually manages to shoot ALEX in the heart.)

GOD. Oh well.
ALEX. *(Dying.)* Why have you forsaken me mighty Lord?
GOD. I tried. I told him not to shoot you but he wouldn't listen. Be thankful that I didn't have you nailed to a cross and have you bleed to death for three days. Now that's pain. We'll have a long talk about it when you come up to heaven. You should be here in about thirty seconds.
ALEX. Thank you

(He dies.)

TYRONE. C'mon. Let's go.

(SHANIQUA and TYRONE EXIT out of the window.)

End Scene

Scene 13

(At rise JOHN is alone on stage reading the bible.)

GOD. John!
JOHN. *(Jumping from his chair.)* Yes Lord!

PROPHET

GOD. Alex has been martyred! He was killed by that drug dealing nigger Tyrone!
JOHN. Oh No!

(He starts to cry.)

GOD. Stop crying! Have some backbone! You must take Alex's place. You are the new Prophet.
JOHN. But Lord-
GOD. But nothing. This is your destiny. You will lead mankind to salvation!
JOHN. Thank you mighty lord.

(He starts to sit down again.)

GOD. John!
JOHN. Here I am!
GOD. Oh. I was afraid that you had left. *(Pause. JOHN starts to sit down.)* John!
JOHN. Here I am gracious lord!
GOD. Take your daughter, your only daughter, whom you love and go to the region of Short Hills. Sacrifice her there as a burnt offering on one of the mountains I will tell you about.
JOHN. I don't think I understand.
GOD. Take your little bitch, and stab her then burn her!
JOHN. But Why? I've done my best to do your bidding.
GOD. Remember how I tested Abraham by telling him to sacrifice his only son Issac?
JOHN. Yes.
GOD. This is your test you moron. Now go on. Kill that little bitch as an offering to me. I love offerings.
JOHN. *(Calls up to his daughter.)* Lisa Honey!

PROPHET

LISA. Yes daddy.

(She ENTERS the room.)

JOHN. You want to take a little drive with daddy?
LISA. Sure! Where are we going to go?
JOHN. Where do you want to go?
LISA. I want to get some ice cream and then go to the toy store.
JOHN. Then that's what we'll do.
LISA. Yaay! Ice cream and the toy store.

(JOHN gathers some rope and a knife and they start to leave when MADELINE ENTERS.)

MADELINE. Where do you think you're going?
JOHN. We're going to get some ice cream.
MADELINE. I already told you. You're not going anywhere with our daughter.
JOHN. You can't stop me.
MADELINE. Yes I can.

(JOHN punches her in the face. She is knocked out on the floor.)

LISA. Daddy no! You killed mommy!
JOHN. Don't worry honey. Mommy's going to be fine. Sometimes daddies must do that to mommies to put mommies in their place. O.K.
LISA. O.K.
JOHN. C'mon. Let's go get that ice cream.
LISA. Yaaay!

End Scene

PROPHET

Scene 14

(At rise LISA and JOHN are walking in the woods.)

LISA. Daddy, where are we? I'm scared.
JOHN. I thought it would be fun to take a little stroll through the woods.
LISA. I thought we were going to the toy store.
JOHN. We will. Don't worry.
LISA. Daddy? Will you give me a piggy back ride?

(SHE jumps on his back and HE starts galloping around like a horse. SHE giggles.)

JOHN. Do you like riding the horsey?
LISA. Yaay! The horsey's fun. Gallop higher! *(He does.)* Yaay!
GOD. John!
JOHN. Here I am.
GOD. What the fuck are you doing?! *(JOHN is sad and silent and looks upwards. Not knowing what to do.)* Obey my command! Kill that little bitch!
LISA. *(Crying.)* Daddy, what is that? It's scary.
JOHN. It's O.K. honey.

(He hugs her and calms her down.)

LISA. Who was talking?
JOHN. That was god honey. Sometimes he can sound scary, but he's really kind and loving and will always protect us as long as we do his bidding.
LISA. He didn't sound so nice.
JOHN. But he is. Trust me. He gave his only son so that we

could be saved. Now lay here honey.

(HE ties HER up.)

LISA. Daddy, what are you doing? I'm scared.
JOHN. There's nothing to be scared of. *(He kisses her on the forehead.)* I love you honey. I love you more that anything in the world. Now close your eyes.

(HE takes out the knife and is holding it over HER in a stabbing position, looking up to GOD hoping that HE will intervene. JOHN is uncertain.)

GOD. Have faith in me John. Obey my holy command.

LISA. *(Opens her eyes.)* Daddy Stop! Don't stab me!

GOD. Do it!

LISA. Daddy, please. Daddy, stop. Daddy, I love you.

GOD. Do it!

(JOHN stabs LISA, SHE screams. Then all is silent. JOHN is crying over his daughter.)

GOD. Well done, John. She's up here with me now, holding my Son's hand. Well done. You passed the test.

End Of Play

47

PROPHET

I'm Gonna Marry A Negress
(from *Prophet*)

words by Thomas Bradshaw · music by Lois Dilivio

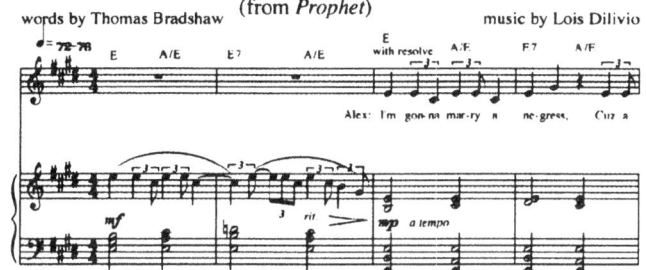

© 2005

PROPHET

I'm Gonna Marry A Negress

PROPHET

I'm Gonna Marry A Negress

PROPHET

I'm Gonna Marry A Negress

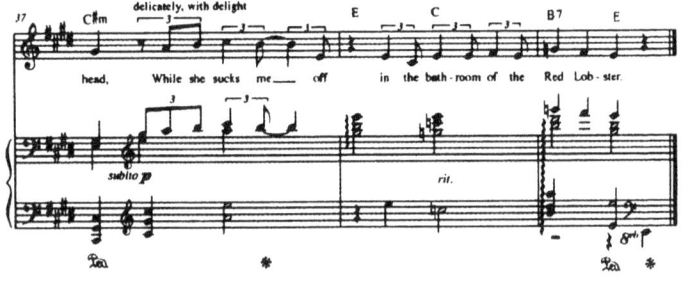

PROPHET

Help Me
from *Prophet*

words by Thomas Bradshaw
music by Lois Dilivio

PROPHET

PROPHET

PROPHET

PROPHET

PROPHET

PROPHET

Oh How Sweet
(from *Prophet*)

words by Thomas Bradshaw
music by Lois Dilivio

58

PROPHET

PROPHET

PROPHET

PROPHET

PROPHET

PROPHET

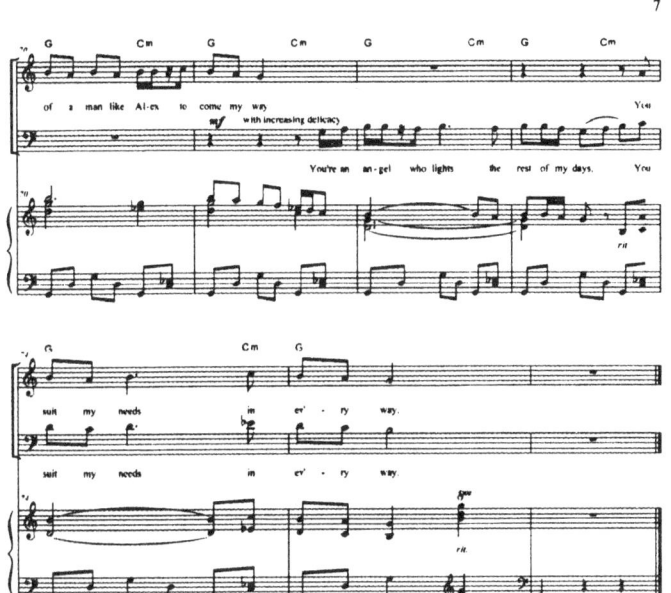

ABOUT THE PLAYWRIGHT

Thomas Bradshaw's play entitled *Purity* was produced at Performance Space 122 in January 2007 and his plays *Strom Thurmond Is Not A Racist* and *Cleansed* were produced on a double bill at The Brick Theatre in February '07. *Strom/Cleansed* have been nominated for Outstanding Original Full Length Script by the 2007 New York Innovative Theater Awards. He has been featured in *The New York Times*, as one of *Time Out New York's* ten playwrights to watch, and as one of *Paper Magazine's* 2006 Beautiful People. His play entitled *Prophet* was presented at P.S. 122 in December 2005. *Strom Thurmond Is Not A Racist* won The American Theater Coop's 2005 National Playwriting Contest. He was a fellow at New York Theater Workshop in '06 -'07 and has been a member of Soho Rep's Writer/Director Lab as well as Lincoln Center's. He performed in the premiere of Richard Maxwell's *The End Of Reality* at The Kitchen in January 2006 and he performed in Young Jean Lee's *Pullman, WA* at P.S. 122 in March 2005. He performed throughout Europe with *The End Of Reality* in the fall of '06. He received his MFA from Mac Wellman's playwriting program and is a Professor at Brooklyn College. Thomas is also the recipient of a 2006 Jerome Foundation Grant.

Also by
Thomas Bradshaw...

Cleansed

Dawn

Purity

Southern Promises

Strom Thurmond is Not a Racist

Please visit our website **samuelfrench.com** for complete descriptions and licensing information.

www.ingramcontent.com/pod-product-compliance
Lightning Source LLC
Chambersburg PA
CBHW071843290426
44109CB00017B/1908